Hodder Gibson

Scottish Examination Materials

ENGLISH
Language Skills

for
**Higher Level
Marking Schemes**

Mary M Firth
Andrew G Ralston

Hodder Gibson

www.hoddereducation.co.uk

INTRODUCTION

This set of photocopiable masters provides suggested answers for all the 'For Practice' exercises in *Language Skills for Higher English* and for the four 'Writing in Focus' extracts. In addition, more detailed marking guidelines are supplied for the four full-length interpretation papers. Obviously, these answers are simply suggestions, and other possibilities exist.

In addition to providing guidance for the use of the exercises in class, these marking schemes could also be copied for students' own use, which might be of particular benefit to those who need extra practice in interpretation work.

MMF / AGR

CONTENTS

Orders: please contact Bookpoint Ltd, 130 Milton Park, Abingdon, Oxon OX14 4SB. Telephone: (44) 01235 827720. Fax: (44) 01235 400454. Lines are open from 9.00 - 6.00, Monday to Saturday, with a 24 hour message answering service. You can also order through our website www.hoddereducation.co.uk.

British Library Cataloguing in Publication Data
A catalogue record for this title is available from the British Library

ISBN-10: 0 7169 32377
ISBN-13: 978 0 7169 32376

Published by Hodder Gibson, 2a Christie Street, Paisley PA1 1NB.
Tel: 0141 848 1609; Fax: 0141 889 6315; Email: hoddergibson@hodder.co.uk
First Published 1999
Impression number   12 11 10 9 8 7 6 5 4
Year   2010 2009 2008 2007 2006 2005

Copyright © 1999 Mary M Firth and Andrew G Ralston

Printed by Hobbs the Printers, Totton, Hants for Hodder Gibson, 2a Christie Street, Paisley, PA1 1NB, Scotland, UK

PART 1 — READING SKILLS

I : UNDERSTANDING THE MEANING

USING YOUR OWN WORDS

FOR PRACTICE — Language Skills (Page 7)

1. *Give **four** changes in his appearance that Jim notices when he looks at himself in the mirror.*

    (2 marks)

    Jim's hair had grown longer;
    his skin tone was sallow and unhealthy;
    his clothes were torn; he was extremely thin;
    he was much wiser looking.
    (Any four; ½ mark for each point.) **Total: 2 marks**

2. (i) *What was the nature of agricultural work during the author's childhood?*   (2 marks)

    Work was extremely hard and physically demanding;
    work was done by hand without the help of machines;
    it involved frustrating waits for good weather and plants to grow.
    (Any two; 1 mark for each.) **Total: 2 marks**

    (ii) *What further clues are there to village life at that time?*   (3 marks)

    Villages were very isolated;
    contact was made on foot or by horse and cart;
    people rarely visited, and only if the visit was strictly essential;
    life was very slow, with no motorised vehicles.
    (Any three; 1 mark for each.) **Total: 3 marks**

3. *Explain why the author found Barcelona astonishing.*   (4 marks)

    The workers were in control of the city, something the author had never experienced before;
    all large buildings were covered in red flags or the Anarchists' own flag;
    walls were all covered in graffiti — hammer and sickle emblems and the initials of the political parties in power;
    the churches were all destroyed;
    the sacred contents of the churches had been burnt.
    (Any four; 1 mark for each.) **Total: 4 marks**

4. (i) *Why, according to the author, was Tintoretto unsatisfied with Titian's work?*

    (3 marks)

    Tintoretto was bored with the simplicity of Titian's shapes and colours;
    he felt Titian's paintings were attractive but did not stir the emotions;
    he felt Titian's paintings were incapable of bringing the great stories of the Bible to life.
    (1 mark for each point.) **Total: 3 marks**

    (ii) *What was Tintoretto's own aim in portraying Bible stories?*   (1 mark)

    His aim was to make the viewer feel excited and moved by the scenes he painted. (1)
    Total: 1 mark

5.   (i)   *What was noteworthy about the winter of 1542?*   (2 marks)

It was very severe;
the weather was stormy and there was deep snow and hard frost.
(2 marks for a detailed answer.)   **Total: 2 marks**

    (ii)   *Identify five political problems that were facing Scotland.*   (10 marks)

Scotland had just been severely beaten by England at the battle of Solway Moss;
many of the most eminent Scottish noblemen were killed at Solway Moss, after their numbers had already been seriously depleted at the battle of Flodden only a generation earlier;
many other important Scottish noblemen were prisoners of the English;
those surviving noblemen in Scotland had a tendency to quarrel among themselves, and were only interested in personal gain;
the Scottish Church, which was still Catholic, was riven by the struggle between those who wished to reform the church from within and those who wished to follow the English example and break away from Rome;
the King was dying and unwilling or unable to confront the problems.
(Any five, sufficiently detailed; 2 marks per point.)   **Total: 10 marks**

CONTEXT QUESTIONS

FOR PRACTICE — Language Skills (Page 10)

Give the meaning of the expressions printed in italics in the following examples and show how the context helped you to arrive at the meaning.

1.   *'implacable' means relentless.*   (1 mark)

The context shows this by saying Silverstein had searched for years to avenge his father (½ mark) and when he found the man on whom he wished to be revenged he 'showed no mercy'. (½ mark)
      Total: 2 marks

2.   *'vacillated' means to swither between two options.*   (1 mark)

The word 'hesitation' means this (½ mark) and the question revealing the two alternatives shows what he was trying to make up his mind about. (½ mark)
      Total: 2 marks

3.   *'minorities': monarchies in which a 'minor' — someone under 21 — is nominally in power.*
      (1 mark)

The clause 'there had been no adult succession since the fourteenth century' shows this as it reveals that for many years a child had succeeded to the throne.   (1 mark)
      Total: 2 marks

4. *'perspective' means the creation of an appearance of depth in a two-dimensional picture.*
(1 mark)

'he shows the figure of the angel in foreshortening' suggests an attempt to make the figure stand out (1 mark); 'geometrical devices suggesting the space on the stage' again is a reference to a 3-D effect (1 mark); 'the illusion of depth' is another way of saying the creation of a three-dimensional effect (1 mark).
(Any two for 2 marks.)   **Total: 3 marks**

5. *'qualified' means partial or incomplete.*   (1 mark)

The reference to the praise of the critics and full houses shows some success for the playwright (1 mark); the references to the later poor audiences and the show's financial problems, 'lucky to break even', show it was not completely successful (1 mark).
                                                                           Total: 3 marks

LINK QUESTIONS

FOR PRACTICE — Language Skills (Page 12)

1. *Show how the first sentence in the second paragraph acts as a link in the argument.*
(2 marks)

The phrase 'illicit grandeurs of her forebears' refers back to the idea of the mother's connections with 'the Castle', and with the noblemen who murdered Edward II (1 mark); the phrase 'quite ordinary poverty' links the idea of the difficult circumstances which follow in detail, such as the girl having to leave school to look after a large family of brothers and sisters because her mother was ill (1 mark).
                                                                           Total: 2 marks

2. *Show how the first sentence of the second paragraph acts as a link in the argument.*
(2 marks)

The phrase 'the position' refers to the stance the beggar had occupied at the end of the drive by the gates (1 mark); 'brought the old man little benefit' introduces in an understated way the information that the old man became too weak to beg, and eventually died of exposure after a snowfall (1 mark).
                                                                           Total: 2 marks

3. *Show how the first sentence of the second paragraph acts as a link in the argument.*
(2 marks)

The phrase 'the appearance' links back to the previous paragraph which was a list of the features of the Queen's beauty (1 mark); and the phrase 'the character of Mary Stuart' introduces a description of her intellect and personality (1 mark).
                                                                           Total: 2 marks

4. *Show how the phrase underlined relates to what has gone before it and introduces a new idea to be developed in the remainder of the paragraph.* (2 marks)

The word 'vast' refers back to the very large numbers working in service (1 mark); the word 'heterogeneous', which means of many different kinds, looks on to the explanation of the huge variety of types of service (1 mark).

Total: 2 marks

5. *Demonstrate that the underlined sentence performs a linking function between the two paragraphs.* (2 marks)

The phrase 'all these qualities' refers back to the list of Einstein's eccentricities such as wearing no socks (1 mark); 'would still not have been sufficient' leads on to what was necessary to make him an international celebrity — 'the missing ingredient' — which was the extreme difficulty of his theory (1 mark).

Total: 2 marks

6. *Show how the sentence in italics acts as a link.* (2 marks)

The phrase 'the years as a golden boy' refers back to the description of Alastair's successful school career (1 mark); the phrase 'made a sad contrast' leads up to the list of disasters which overtook him later, at University (1 mark).

Total: 2 marks

II : APPRECIATING THE STYLE

TACKLING STRUCTURE QUESTIONS

FOR PRACTICE — Language Skills (Page 18)

Comment on the types of sentences and paragraphs used in the following pieces of writing. Then discuss what effects the writers are aiming at.

1. All sentences are short so they can be quickly and easily assimilated by the reader. Most are statements, giving information. The second sentence, almost in command form, is more strongly persuasive. The third paragraph is a section of questions and answers in the form of short statements, many just minor sentences or phrases. This gives the impression of setting up a conversation with the reader, creating a chatty, friendly tone. Paragraphs are short, to make instant impact on the reader. All of these techniques are suited to an advertisement which must get its message across forcefully and economically.

2. Sentences are extremely short. There are some rhetorical questions: 'Who sent for it?' There are some minor sentences, e.g., 'My teachers', and abbreviations, 'didn't'; 'isn't', etc. The subject of many sentences is 'I'. The tone is therefore informal and personal. The impression is of the narrator having an internal dialogue with himself. As this is a novel, the effect is one of extreme realism, and the reader is able to identify closely with the character whose internal thought processes he / she is sharing.

3. The arrangement of the words into lines beginning with a capital letter shows this to be poetry. All the sentences are incomplete; they have no finite verbs and are just a list of descriptive phrases. The ellipsis (. . .) at the end of line three suggests the poet breaking off to observe the 'swallows' more closely. In the fourth line, the number of short phrases, broken up by commas, has a jerky rhythm which imitates the sense of 'a twitch, a twitter'. As the poem progresses the lines get shorter, with one line containing only a single word.

    The first word is in the form of a question. The following six lines seem to be reflecting on this, while the third paragraph answers the question firmly with two exclamations. The exclamation marks and use of italics make these specially forceful. Placing the negative 'never' at the beginning of a line throws emphasis on this part of the answer.

4. Many sentences are in the form of commands, 'Do pay a visit . . .'. The writer is trying to persuade the reader to follow his advice. The use of the future tense in 'you'll be fascinated . . .' continues in this persuasive style. The use of the second person, 'you', is colloquial as it sets up a conversational tone with the reader. There are also statements which give information. The last line of the entry is in note form. The bold type in 'open' draws attention to this being an important piece of information for the reader. It is followed by a colon which introduces the exact times and days.

5. The first paragraph is a series of statements, most of which begin with the subject 'he', followed by a verb: 'turned'; 'read'; 'saw'. This repetition of the structure is deliberately monotonous. The narrative depicts a man reading fairly trivial pieces of information in a newspaper, most of which are to do with money, and the sentences list these. However, the last sentence ends with the phrase 'eight hundred thousand pounds'. Placing it last like this creates a sudden climax because it is such a large sum of money.

The next paragraph consists of a repetition of the phrase 'eight hundred thousand'. The fact that the dramatic sum is repeated, the shortness of the phrase, the use of the exclamation mark, and its placement in a paragraph on its own build a yet greater climax and create suspense in the reader.

The extract ends with a simple statement, summing up the character's feelings, which has the effect of relaxing the tension a little.

6. Sentences are short and many are in note form. The layout with days and times shows this to be an extract from a diary. It is written in a typically abbreviated diary style, omitting some personal pronouns, verbs and articles: 'was just leaving . . .'; 'unexpected surprise'; 'card is still here.' The use of colloquialisms, 'Humph', adds to the informality of the style.

7. There is frequent use of repetition: 'louder — louder — louder'; 'no, no', etc., which creates a series of climaxes. The use of dashes, exclamation marks and italics are devices which make the climaxes stand out even more. There are many exclamations and rhetorical questions which create a very emotional, excitable tone. In the last sentence of the first paragraph, the syntax breaks down completely and becomes incoherent. The dash at the end of the first paragraph indicates a breaking off of thought. The passage obviously shows the outpourings of a very disturbed mind which culminates in the outburst of direct speech in the second paragraph.

    There are several archaisms: 'they heard not'; 'dissemble no more'; which reveal this writing is not of the present day.

PUNCTUATION

FOR PRACTICE — Language Skills (Pages 22–23)

1. Use of colon to introduce a list.

2. Use of semicolon to show link between two halves of sentence, the second half being a consequence of the first.

3. Semicolon creates a contrast between the two halves of the sentence.

4. In the first sentence the colon introduces a list of colours. In the second sentence, semicolons are used to split up the items in the list.

5. Use of a dash to add on an extra piece of information.

6. Semicolon used to create contrast between the two parts of the sentence.

7. Words contained between the two dashes are examples of the things that 'interested me.' An example of parenthesis.

8. Semicolons split up the description into its different aspects: mountains, trees, fields, etc.

9. Parentheses used to allow the author to put in her own feelings and reactions in the midst of the description; repeated use of dashes indicates a sense of rapid thought and excitement.

10. Colon introduces a list of alternative explanations, each of which is separated from the one that follows by a semicolon. Dash used to add on an extra piece of information.

SENTENCE STRUCTURE

FOR PRACTICE (Pages 27–28)

1. Use of repetition (series of expressions on the pattern of a verb followed by the word 'any' followed by a noun). These are arranged in ascending order of importance, building up to a climax. Antithesis is also used ('support / oppose' and 'friend / foe').

2. Series of exclamations designed to show a feeling of relief and elation.

3. First sentence is a rhetorical question, which is a more effective way of putting over the point as no-one would be likely to say that they would prefer to be slaves than free men. The sentence is also an example of antithesis, as it contains balanced opposites ('living' versus 'dead' and 'die all slaves' versus 'live all free men'). The second sentence is a list divided up by semicolons, again arranged in ascending order, climaxing in 'I slew him'.

4. An example of antithesis. 'Worse' contrasts with 'better' and 'should not have been invited' contrasts with 'should not have come'. Structures are parallel / symmetrical in that both subordinate clauses begin with 'if' and both principal clauses begin with 'I'.

5. This extract aims to create suspense by keeping the identity of 'something different' until the short sentence at the end ('It was a girl'). The last sentence is deliberately short to contrast with the longer one preceding it.

6. The whole extract is basically an expansion of the short opening statement, 'Fog everywhere'. This is a 'minor sentence' as it contains no verb which gives added impact. The constant repetition of the word 'fog' emphasises how it worked its way into every aspect of the scene, from the large areas of landscape to the smallest craft on the river. The verb 'is' is omitted in all the principal clauses.

7. An example of climax. The build-up is assisted by the use of alliteration on the letter 'c'. The disagreements between mother and daughter escalate from criticisms to corrections and end up with violence ('I even threw her own china at her.')

8. Another list building up to a climax ('be free one day'). The length of the list also effectively conveys how long and difficult the struggle will be before this freedom is finally achieved. The quotation comes from a speech by Martin Luther King.

9. Although the second sentence beginning with 'but' could have been joined to the first, it is separated in order to create a greater contrast between ''generous' and 'prudent'. The words 'he now had four children' are in parenthesis. A colon is used to introduce the 'two factors'. The last sentence contains an element of balance and could therefore be said to make use of antithesis.

10. The colon is used to introduce a list of all the different types of dancers. The list is arranged as a series of antitheses (gracefully, awkwardly, etc.). The second sentence is split into short sections divided by semicolons. Each section describes a stage in the dance, thus conveying an idea of regular, rhythmical movements.

INFORMAL LANGUAGE, DIALECT AND JARGON

FOR PRACTICE — Language Skills (Pages 33–34)

(a) **Informal, conversational language**
Expressions such as: 'Good heavens!', 'I'm afraid so', 'Of course I am'.

(b) **Dialect**
E.g., 'He's a gawp', 'the great lubbert', 'knows nowt'.

(c) **Jargon**
Words such as 'myxoedema', 'hypothyroidism' and 'bradycardia'.

Questions on the effectiveness of imagery ('For Practice', pp. 39–40)

1. Comparison of the house to a dinosaur suggests various similarities: it is obsolete; it takes up a great deal of space; it consumes a great deal; and so on. The comparison to a fossil continues the idea of something prehistoric lingering on into the modern age. Both are examples of metaphors.

2. Personification. Cranes are said to have human attributes ('How noble we are') and physical characteristics ('to drink at the river'; 'turning their long necks'). There is a play on words here, as a crane is also a type of bird.

3. 'Putted' imitates the irregular flickering of the gas and as such has an onomatopoeic effect. 'Like a sick man's heart' suggests the irregular flutter of a dying man's heart. The simile 'mysterious as a chapel' introduces the idea of a religious atmosphere continued by other similes which follow ('tapers', 'icons', etc.). A number of the descriptive effects here are based on the contrast of light and dark.

4. Two similes compare pleasures to flowers and to snow, the link being that these only last for a short time. Both the moment of happiness and the beauty of the flower and of the snow pass away quickly.

5. This extract depends on an extended metaphor comparing the guitar instructor to a doctor. His guitar-case is compared to a doctor's bag; he asks the 'patient' how he is feeling; he tests his co-ordinations and gives him exercises as if they were a prescription. The exercises will cure the pupil's faulty co-ordination just as the prescription will cure the patient's illness.

6. Here the poet uses a simile which compares the tough American policeman to a gorilla. A gorilla, of course, is hardly a timid animal; for the poet to say that the policeman is 'less timid' than a gorilla must therefore mean that he is very tough indeed. The metaphor 'thin tissue over violence' suggests that even when the streets are quiet the threat of violence is always just below the surface; a thin tissue is only a very fragile covering which can easily be torn off.

7. Describing the Earl as 'drooping like a wet sock' is highly comical. It is an example of hyperbole as a wet sock is obviously much more droopy than a person could be. It suggests a stooping, languid figure who appears to have no backbone and who is rather ridiculous.

8. 'Skewer like' is appropriate as a skewer is long, thin and associated with piercing meat. This makes the dagger seem lethal and horrific. 'Like a hen' suggests the frantic fluttering a hen makes when picked up or frightened, and reveals the victim's panic. It also shows him as a rather pathetic, defenceless figure, lacking in dignity or courage. 'Like so much sawdust' emphasises the inertness of the dead body. Sawdust would be shapeless and lifeless; it also has no value. It is associated with stuffed dolls, also suggesting lifelessness.

9. The comparison of the rain to glass splinters effectively conveys how sharp and penetrating the rain was and suggests it hit the people with such force that it was almost like a series of physical attacks. It also has connotations of pain: being wounded by glass splinters would be extremely painful.

10. Personification of time as a magician. A magician appears to make amazing transformations; in the same way, places can be altered beyond recognition over a period of time.

FOR PRACTICE, — Language Skills (Pages 44–45)

1. Onomatopoeia. To the poet the words 'hush' and 'west' sound like the tyres of the bus going through puddles on the wet road.

2. Pun on the word 'arms': (i) limbs, (ii) weapons of war.

3. Alliteration creates a link between the various aspects of the description, suggesting, for instance, that the 'confetti' was mixed in with the 'crowd'.

4. Onomatopoeia: personification of 'sobs' and 'drool'.

5. Alliteration of the letter 'm' — appropriate because it strengthens the idea of a dark, monotonous scene. There is also an example of antithesis after the colon.

6. Pun on 'ties': (i) articles of clothing often used as Christmas gifts for men and (ii) girls are unattached and are looking for a permanent relationship which they hope to achieve by buying a gift for someone.

7. 'Fruitless fruits': an oxymoron. The poet is thinking of fruit which is commonly given to hospital patients by their visitors. The fruit is 'fruitless' in that it will not be of any help to the patient.

8. Hyperbole, used for a humorous effect.

9. Member of Parliament speaks in emotive language (e.g., 'savage cuts'). The Government Minister replies in a formal style which tries to make the measures less severe (e.g., '. . . to see if economies can be made.'). This is an example of euphemism or circumlocution.

10. 'Interment' is a euphemism for 'buried' while 'incineration' is a euphemism for 'cremated'.

11. Words such as 'thou', 'heartily do I wish', etc., identify this extract as an example of archaic language.

12. A parody of sports journalism, employing many clichés typical of the genre such as 'a game of two halves', 'flirted with disaster', 'pull the trigger', and so on.

13. The humour of this passage derives from the fact that the author identifies circumlocution being used in the menu's description of the dishes available ('Cumbrian Air Dried Ham', etc.) and then imitates and extends this in increasingly exaggerated ways: e.g., 'horizontal walking surface anterior to my feet' which simply means the floor. The passage ends with an effective anti-climax, contrasting the previous 'inflated language' with the 'no-nonsense' simplicity of 'Sweets Menu'.

FOR PRACTICE — Language Skills (Page 49)

The whole argument that the Circumlocution Office was 'the most important Department under Government' is ironic. The placing in parenthesis of the words 'as everybody knows without being told' makes clear that the author means exactly the opposite.

The humour of the notion that the imagined Gunpowder Plot could not have been stopped until vast amounts of paperwork had been done first — even when the match was due to be lit in half an hour — alerts us to the hyperbole of the list which follows ('half a bushel of minutes', etc.). Note also the climax in the last sentence of paragraph one as the quantities progress from half a bushel to several sacks to a family-vault full.

By the second paragraph the reader will have grasped the ironic tone and will therefore see that expressions like 'glorious establishment', 'bright revelation', 'shining influence', 'delicate perception' and so on are meant to convey precisely the opposite.

EMOTIVE LANGUAGE

FOR PRACTICE — Language Skills (Page 51)

This is the opening of a newspaper article in which a journalist described an interview with disgraced Olympic skater Tonya Harding. Can you pick out the ways in which the writer uses emotive language to capture the reader's interest?

Why Tonya the wicked witch is still running from her past

Commentary:

In the title, the phrase 'wicked witch' evokes hatred. The alliteration has impact; 'witch' suggests a more than human degree of evil.

In the first paragraph, 'like a fugitive', 'nervously scanning' and 'on the run' build up an impression of furtiveness which causes us to dislike and distrust Tonya. 'Notorious past' hints at wickedness and prevents any sympathy being aroused by her plight.

'The scent of scandal clings like cheap perfume' is an image which appeals to the senses. The idea of 'cheap' perfume invites us to share the author's evaluation of Tonya as common and low class.

In the third paragraph there are words suggesting very strong hatred and condemnation: 'loathed and vilified'. Further extreme terms which arouse the reader's feelings are 'violent', 'monstrous greed' and 'cowardly'. 'Cripple' is also an emotive way to describe the attack on her rival, with its associations of disablement which conversely arouses sympathy for Tonya's victim. The hyperbole in the last line, 'Americans turn crimson with shame', emphasises the dislike in which Tonya is held.

The whole article is very one-sided, with no attempt to consider Tonya Harding's side of the story or to look at the matter coolly and objectively.

FURTHER PRACTICE (Page 51)

In the following extracts, pick out words and phrases which contribute to the tone. Say what the tone is and explain how the language chosen conveys it. Comment on any features of the language which reinforce the tone, such as euphemism, oxymoron, hyperbole, unusual juxtapositions, emotive language and so on.

1. The tone is humorous throughout, mocking the absurdities of techniques used in this TV show such as slow motion to represent action. He uses a list of oxymorons to emphasise this absurdity: 'action numbers at glacial speed'; 'supreme burst of lethargy'. The writer also mocks the clichés of the genre: 'heavies'; 'sad cello weeping on the sound-track'. He uses a humorous anticlimax after the list of sentences beginning mock-formally with 'one . . .' He ends with an example of bathos (ludicrous anticlimax): 'One thinks one is being had.' His use of colloquialisms expresses his frustration at the silliness of the plot: 'why can't the soft twit . . .' His deliberately down-to-earth language 'clobber the foe' contrasts humorously with the pretentiousness of the programme's language: 'in quest of a way to control the raging spirit . . .'. The last comment is full of irony: 'he will be a long time on the trail.'

2. An emotive tone is used to present the plight of the poor servants. The writer uses words or phrases expressing strong emotion: 'miserable'; 'wretched'. The hyperbole of 'in bondage' is also very effective. Alliteration is used to emphasise the abject conditions of the poor servants: 'sleeping on a sack under the stairs'. He also contrasts the prosperity of the rich servants to stress the poverty of the unfortunate ones and arouse sympathy for them.

3. A series of rhetorical questions in the second paragraph creates an angry, polemical mood. Its hectoring tone is reminiscent of a political speech. Putting 'progress' in inverted commas is ironic and contributes to the serious, critical feeling. This tone is aimed at stirring up indignation in the reader by sounding angry and using scaremongering tactics.

4. A strongly emotive tone aims at provoking sympathy for the abandoned dog. An outburst of short sentences conveys the rage of the writer: 'so that was it'. Words expressing his extreme feelings such as 'murderous rage' and 'physically sick' invite the reader to share his anger. Very vivid words are chosen to depict the abuse of the dog: 'dumped'; 'hurled'. He presents the heartlessness of the owners in a very bitter, ironic tone: 'driven merrily away'; 'had they laughed, I wondered'. The words which describe the dog are extremely sentimental: 'bewildered little creature'; 'toiling vainly'. These wring sympathy from the reader.

5. This extract has a humorous tone. The extremely simplistic language 'there was a man' prepares us for an absurd dialogue which continues in this tongue-in-cheek tone. The extended personification of the bicycle is deliberately ridiculous, 'don't do that; you'll hurt it'; 'it had not done anything to him'. The repetition of 'wobble' also becomes comical because of the onomatopoeia.

6. The writer uses an ironic tone here to express his disapproval of the natives' bloodthirstiness in wishing to see an elephant shot. In the expression 'he was merely ravaging their homes,' 'merely' is ironic as this is obviously serious yet they were unconcerned; it is only the prospect of blood which arouses them: 'it was a bit of fun to them.' The author's irony is bitter and reveals his distaste for their callous attitude.

7. The language of the direct speech is very extreme. Many words indicating strong emotions are used: 'sick to my guts'; 'you and your twisted mouthings'; 'sickened'; 'revolted'. Yet some of the language is very high-flown: 'a heritage of shame'. The language aims at being emotive but the combination of the two styles lessens the impact and seems artificial. The number of words indicating disgust is excessive and actually makes it less effective by being overdone. This is an example of writing where the writer's skill is shown to be inadequate to the task of producing the desired tone.

8. The first two pieces of dialogue are delivered in a neutral tone: they form a simple statement and question.

    However, the third paragraph is heavily ironic. It appears to be full of praise: 'your native shrewdness'; 'that innate cunning'; 'the delight of your friends'; but this is undercut by pointing out the extreme stupidity of the question: 'enclosing cipher and message in the same envelope.' The tone is one of withering ridicule, though perhaps 'dear' in 'my dear Watson' is a genuine word of endearment!

9. The tone of the first sentence is one of sincere approval: 'spry' and 'hard working' are both complimentary. However, the second sentence moves into ironic mode. The author is imitating the shocked and prejudiced comments people make about the washerwoman and her daughters. The short sentences and colloquial language, 'awful', 'gaolbird', show she is giving examples of actual remarks. There is a double irony here. Some of the remarks themselves are ironic in that they mean the opposite of the actual words: 'Very nice company . . .', but the author's use of parody exposes the prejudice and cruelty behind the comments.

10. The tone of this extract is 'tongue-in-cheek'. The absurdity of the name 'Pookworthy' followed by a list of apparently academic letters shows this is a spoof. The author is pretending to write a preface to a great work of literature, apologising for the fact that she has been a journalist.

    Her use of high-flown language mocks writers who are pretentious and take themselves over-seriously: 'the lovely polishing of every grave and lucent phrase.' She is being ironic when she appears to criticise writing in short sentences and says she will learn to make her sentences 'as long as possible'. In the second paragraph she produces a sentence eighty-eight words long in humorous imitation of the turgid style of these 'serious' writers. She also mocks the prejudice so-called 'serious' writers have against journalists: 'the life of a journalist is nasty, brutish and short.'

11. She pokes fun at obtuse critics with her ridiculous idea of having a star system, as in a tourist guide, to point out the 'finer passages' in her novel. The colloquialism of 'sheer flapdoodle' is very down to earth and contrasts with 'Literature' which is given a capital 'L' ironically to mock the reverence with which some critics treat particular books. The extreme simplicity of her last sentence contrasts humorously with the excessive ornateness of the parody.

III: IDENTIFYING THE PURPOSE

GENRE

FOR PRACTICE (Page 59)

Each of the following pieces of writing belongs to a particular genre. In pairs or small groups, read and discuss each extract and then write a short report. Pick out ideas and language features which help you to identify *(a)* the genre and *(b)* the intended readership. Then *(c)* mention any additional features of the writing which seem in any way special.

1. This is a non-fiction book on the subject of Physics. This can be told from references to 'protons and neutrons'; 'quarks'; the mention of a real life physicist and a real institution, Caltech. Since it does not contain any formulae or mathematical symbols it seems to be a book *about* Physics, rather than *on* Physics. The discussion of the derivation and pronunciation of the term 'quark', with a reference to a humorous quotation from James Joyce, suggests the book is aimed at the layman rather than the Physicist. Thus it would come into the genre of popular science which aims to make a specialist subject entertaining to the general public. It does, however, presuppose an educated readership who would have heard of James Joyce and who would be able to take in the rather complicated description of the various types of quark.

2. This is an extract from a fictional story since it involves animals who behave like humans. The mouse 'made a curtsey' which suggests she is wearing clothes. The simplicity of the sentence structures and paragraphing suggests it is intended for young children. The rhythmical repetition of the 'tip tap etc.' is the kind of thing very young children would enjoy. The reference to 'little' things such as the 'funny little noises' and the 'little lady mouse' would also appeal.

    It could be assumed this story is not of the present century because of the archaic language: 'pipkins'; 'wainscot'. The style of the direct speech, 'this is very peculiar', is rather too stiff and formal for the present day. The description of the setting with the dresser and the mouse's curtsey also suggest another era.

3. The opening sentence sets the tone of black comedy. The idea is so bizarre and ridiculous and the expression so blunt that this extract must be fiction. This is confirmed by the introduction of characters and a fictitious place name, Gallanach. The comic tone is immediately consolidated by the picture of the uncle 'snoring in harmony to Bach's B-minor mass'. A feature of the writing is the use of highly comical incongruous comparisons: the mother's hat is 'like a flying saucer', the father's ears were waggling like 'John Wayne's shoulders'. The narrative is told in the first person in a racy, flippant style. The idea of using a funeral service as a setting for comedy might shock some people, and so this author is probably someone who would mainly write for a young audience who would appreciate this outrageous style of humour. It is high quality, extremely entertaining writing.

4. This is non-fiction; autobiography / personal memoir. The author is describing her Chinese grandmother and, in particular, the ordeal of foot-binding. This is a real piece of social history, and the Chinese reference and quotation gives it authority as non-fiction. (It might be noted that sometimes this genre is imitated in fiction.) It is aimed at the general reader rather than the specialist historian as such a personal account is made to be exciting and moving — 'my grandmother screamed in agony' — rather than merely informative. The Chinese translations, such as 'three-inch golden lilies', are poetic and appealing to lovers of good writing.

5. This is a story from Greek mythology. It is a third person narrative and includes direct speech. The paragraphs and sentences are fairly short and the vocabulary simple and colloquial: 'partied'; 'who'd'. These features, and the simplicity of the syntax, e.g., 'It was a horse . . .' shows it is intended for children. It is, however, aimed at older children who would be amused by the colloquialism of 'free booze'. The writing is humorous in its use of deliberately anachronistic details such as the description of Helen's 'boyfriend' with his 'permed blonde hair and chunky jewellery'. Also amusing to older children who already knew of the Trojan horse would be the boyfriend's response of 'ridiculous' to Helen's intelligent suggestion that it might be a trick.

6. This extract is non-fiction. It is discursive and reflective and considers the topic of social class. It is also personal: 'when I went shooting . . .'. Its purpose is both to inform and entertain. Its serious purpose is to describe the mores of the English aristocrat, but it is written in a very humorous style. The two anecdotes in the last paragraph are highly comic and almost certainly apocryphal. The style also achieves humour in the occasional use of slang: 'not caring a stuff', which contrasts with the more formal language used: 'a rich vein of eccentricity'. The difficulty of some of the language, and the Shakespearean reference suggests this book is aimed at the well-educated general adult reader.

7. This extract is narrative in style and is clearly fiction. It is set in a castle, and characters, Emily and Annette, are named. The setting suggests it might fall into the genre of romance / thriller, and this is confirmed by its references to a 'veiled picture' and 'the late lady of the castle'; 'mystery' and 'terror'. The extract ends on a 'cliff-hanger' when the character of Emily 'dropped senseless to the floor'. Its aim is to intrigue and thrill the reader. The writer builds up suspense successfully. A good example is in the last sentence of the extract, where a series of short clauses broken up by commas leads to a climax. The difficulty of the language suggests this is a novel aimed at adult lovers of romance / thriller.

Many features of the style indicate this is a pre-twentieth century writer. The paragraphs are denser and the sentences longer and more complex than would be found in a contemporary thriller. Much of the diction has an archaic formality: 'melancholy', 'edifice', 'recollection', and there are some usages which would not be used today: 'of uncommon size'; 'the chamber.' The setting of 'ancient grandeur' in the castle and features such as the 'veil', the reference to 'terror' and the swooning of the heroine place this in the specific category of Gothic romance.

8. This extract refers to real places — 'Butlin's, Minehead' — which suggests it is non-fiction, and it is told in the first person. It is therefore from the broad genre of personal memoir / autobiography. The fact that it is describing a place and clearly from a foreigner's point of view — 'I had not seen flimsier buildings in England' — places it in the more specific genre of travel writing. The reference to 'a Polish joke' suggests the writer is American, as these are the equivalent of 'Irish' jokes in Britain. The aim is clearly to entertain as well as to inform as the tone is sardonic and mocking. The extreme nature of the criticism eventually becomes comic: 'they were so ugly . . .' The writer describes the holiday camp in terms of a military encampment, which is presumably — at least to some extent — hyperbole: 'barracks-like buildings'. The style is not particularly demanding and seems to be aimed at the general adult reader.

9. This is obviously science fiction, showing many of the clichés of the genre. It includes outlandish names for extra-terrestrials: 'the Cyrastorian', 'Gezra'; while humans are called 'Earthman' or 'Earth creature'. There are references to 'deep space' and 'the space-craft'. Technology seems far advanced: 'the screen which panned up images', and the extra-terrestrials consider the Earth and its inhabitants 'primitive'. Also typical of the genre is the portrayal of a society which is chillingly de-humanised, where people are treated like machines: 'a memory wipe'; 'the Appropriate Behaviour Compliance Elder'.

10. This extract refers to the titles of television programmes, e.g., 'Owner Occupied', and uses television jargon: 'pilot show', 'sit-com', 'series'. Obviously it is a television review, as the writer goes on to pass judgement on a programme. Although this reviewer is aiming at humour, and entertaining as well as informing his readers, clear indications of his views on the programme are presented in a subtle and witty way. He finds the fake German accent of one of the leading actors ridiculous, and this is imitated throughout his review in spellings such as 'Cherman', 'luffable' and 'chust'. He also includes more direct jokes such as 'charming the Poles to death'. Much of the language is mocking the clichés familiar from other war films: 'the cuddlesome local beauty'; 'a kind of Hotel Sahara with less sand'. The use of the deliberate vulgarism 'crap' is comic for being unexpected and punctures the pretentiousness of the show. The subtlety of this writing suggests it is aimed at a well-educated adult reader and one might guess, correctly, that it was originally published in a broadsheet newspaper.

11. This extract is narrative, told in the first person. It is describing a battle. References to 'the French', 'barbed-wire entanglements', 'machine guns' and 'the charge' suggests a first world war scenario.

    The author builds up his effects by using short, dramatic sentences and the historic present tense. These lend immediacy and bring the scene to life. They are also typical of fiction, which aims to involve the reader by writing emotively, rather than of real memoirs which would probably use more complex sentences and a simple narrative past tense. The writer engages the reader by various language techniques. He uses onomatopoeia, 'rattle', 'crack', to recreate the sounds of battle. Emotive diction is employed: 'torn to pieces', 'distorted', 'suffered heavily'. Particularly moving is the final horrific anecdote of the dismembered 'stumps of arms' hanging on the wire. The simile 'as though he were praying' is particularly effective as it is both incongruous (there is no time to pray in the heat of battle) and appropriate (men are terrified and pray to survive) at the same time.

12. This is an extract from a guide book, as it starts with a title of a place, and then gives its location: 'off Glasgow Green'. It also includes details of how to see the place and describes its most noteworthy features: 'glazed brick', 'battlements', etc. This is factual writing, aimed at giving information to the prospective tourist.

    The tone is colloquial. This is achieved by the writer's use of exclamation and abbreviation: 'You're not seeing things!' The writer gives the impression of chatting to the reader with a simple question in the form of a phrase, 'The reason?' and the use of colloquialisms like 'Well'. The use of bold type and capitals in 'EXTRA . . . EXTRA . . .' shows the writer is working hard to attract the reader's attention. The simple, direct, colloquial style and the striking typography suggest this would also be accessible to older children.

13. This is narrative writing in the third person. It is fiction, with characters and a setting in a castle. References suggests an adventure genre: 'escaped the various perils', 'the shadow of a man', etc. The setting is atmospheric and adds to the suspense: 'the great arched passage', 'the little winding stair', 'the chambers of Mervyn's Tower'. The style deliberately aims at suspense. In the first sentence, the structure, with a series of phrases detailing the stages of the character's passage through the courtyard, slowly builds suspense. The last sentence of the second paragraph, with the repetition of 'ascended', and the parenthesis to build further tension, ends in an exciting climax: 'suddenly thrown wide open'.

    The language of the narrative is slightly archaic in style, but that of the dialogue much more so with its use of totally archaic forms and structures such as 'art thou', 'sayest thou me so', 'come hither'. This discrepancy would suggest the author is trying to recreate an earlier time, and so this book could be seen to fall into the genre of historical novel.

You will find the actual sources of the extracts in
Appendix II of *Language Skills for Higher English*

PART 2 — WRITING IN FOCUS

The 'Writing in Focus' section (pages 66–79) contains four extracts from contemporary journalism, accompanied by comments and questions focusing on the writers' techniques.

These passages can be used as the basis for class discussion. For example, the class could be divided into groups and one member could report the group's findings back to the whole class.

The passages could also be used for written answers, although the questions differ from those in the formal interpretation practice papers as they are 'open-ended' and no indication is given of how much should be written.

WRITING IN FOCUS (1): Sharon the Shark (Pages 67–70)

Page 68: How does the writer combine humour with serious discussion?

Examples of **alliteration** in paragraphs one and two include *feeding frenzy, finned through its films, hoovering up holidaymakers, film-makers' facts are as false as their rubber fishes, peckish predator, bathing beach babes.*

The writer is deliberately trying to write in an exaggerated 'tabloid' journalistic style, just as the films oversimplify and overdramatise the activities of the sharks.

Imagery

Piscine serial killer: 'piscine' relates to fish, and the expression suggests that sharks are the equivalent of psychopathic mass murderers. An example of hyperbole and personification.

Box offices enjoyed a feeding frenzy: suggests that the box offices 'devoured' their paying customers in the same way as the sharks literally 'devoured' their victims. Alliteration, personification and hyperbole are used here.

The film-makers' facts are as false as their rubber fishes: a simile making use of alliteration for a humorous effect. The author is suggesting that, just as the props used in the films are fake ('rubber fishes'), so too the 'facts' about sharks that the films present are equally untrue.

The peckish predator finds human snacks about as appetising as stale Ryvita: a simile making use of ironic contrast: as stale Ryvita would not be in the least appetising, the writer is really saying that sharks do not enjoy eating people. The alliteration of 'peckish predator' again gives a flippant tone, sending up the kind of dramatic headlines used in tabloid journalism.

Tone:

Paragraphs one and two are flippant / light-hearted / melodramatic.

Paragraph three is more analytical / objective / reflective / thoughtful, as indicated by the use of more complex vocabulary and jargon ('mammalian complicity', 'apex of the ocean food chain', 'marine ecosystem', etc.).

Page 69: How does the writer develop an argument in a series of paragraphs?

Paragraph 3: The writer develops the point that 'the shark is ostracised and misunderstood' by emphasising the following points:
— how little is known about it;
— how it cannot be kept in captivity;
— it may have a key role to play in the 'marine ecosystem'.

Paragraph 4: The writer develops the point that 'the great white shark is now at the margins of extinction' by giving two examples:
— it is now listed as an endangered species;
— large numbers are killed by humans.

Paragraph 5: The writer develops the point that 'surfers and divers run a real risk':
— by giving details of the way that sharks eat their prey;
— by describing how sharp its teeth are;
— by giving examples of electronic devices to protect swimmers from attack.

A new paragraph could have been begun at the words 'But technology is tackling this' as a new aspect of the topic — protective measures — is now being discussed.

Page 70: How does the writer reach an effective conclusion?

Think of two ways in which the last four lines remind you of the opening two paragraphs.

— Use of light-hearted alliteration.
— Returns to the subject of films.

The last sentence sums up the whole point that the writer wants to make. Explain what his point actually is.

— That it is time sharks were presented more sympathetically rather than being stereotyped as killers.

Compare what you have just written with the author's last sentence. Which would have more impact on the reader? Why?

Author's last sentence has more impact because it personifies the shark, thus making it easier for us to be sympathetic to it. 'Sharon the Shark' might even be a possible film title.

WRITING IN FOCUS (2): The Spoils of Childhood (Pages 70–73)

Why are these particular details included?

The particular details of the interior are included to demonstrate how dramatic the layout of the shop is, and how lavish its fittings are.

Why are so many 'ands' used here?

The series of 'ands' emphasises the wide range of goods on sale, as if to suggest that the list is never-ending.

What is the tone of the first sentence of paragraph two?

Tone is conversational. The writer imagines that the reader will mock the ambience of the shop as being artificial and 'trendy'.

What social stereotypes is the author drawing on here?

She refers to stereotypes of the imagined customers: wealthy and fashionable women who usually leave their children to the care of a nanny, or fathers who rarely see their children and try to keep them amused by bribing them with gifts.

These two paragraphs contain straightforward reporting. What differences in the style do you notice compared to the previous two?

Tone changes to a more factual and less ironic reporting style.

Comment on the word choice of 'self-deprecating maverick'.

'Self-deprecating' means taking a modest and self-critical approach rather than boasting.

'Maverick' means someone who is not afraid to be independent and nonconformist. (From a nineteenth-century Texas cattle-owner called Samuel Maverick who did not brand his herd of cattle when other farmers did).

Explain the store owner's philosophy.

The store owner is concerned to make his shops look attractive and to create a welcoming atmosphere and not just to maximise profits. 'Quixotically' means unrealistically romantic, idealistic.

What contrast between the activities of today's children and those of a previous generation is suggested?

The contrast is that in the past children were expected to behave according to adults' wishes whereas today more emphasis is put on allowing children to be themselves.

Why are these particular examples chosen and what point is being made?

Examples of popular activities for today's youngsters (McDonalds, etc.) are contrasted with the 'boring' activities endured by previous generations of children, to stress the much greater variety of fun available today.

Comment on the tone of the last sentence of this paragraph.

The tone of the last sentence is tongue-in-cheek or mock-serious. 'Wearing school shoes in the holidays' is not really a shocking or extraordinary thing to do, but it is presented as if it is. The 1960s were not really so long ago as to be a 'dark' age.

Explain the function of the colon.

The colon introduces the reason for the point made in the first part of the sentence.

How does the short sentence act as a turning point in the argument?

The short sentence 'but we do' turns the argument away from parental criticisms of the young being commercially exploited towards a discussion of why parents are in fact quite happy to go along with this process for their own reasons.

In your own words, explain why adults want to buy gifts and treats for children, basing your answer on the last two paragraphs.

Adults want to buy gifts for children (i) because they enjoy seeing the happiness that such gifts bring to the young; (ii) because adults worry about the dangerous world in which their young are growing up and try to compensate by buying escapist pleasures for their children.

'Gild the cage' is an example of a metaphor. What is being compared to what? Think about the implications of this comparison.

> The children's rooms are compared to the cages in which animals are kept. Just as these cages might be 'gilded' (i.e. brightly decorated) so that they do not give an impression of imprisonment, in the same way parents will provide entertaining equipment like television and computers so that their children do not realise they are being kept indoors away from the threatening outside world.

Title:
> The pun is that 'spoils' can refer both to the material gains / rewards / benefits of childhood and to the way that childhood is being 'spoiled' or ruined. The title also make us think of the expression 'spoilt child'.

Objective or Subjective: Approach is generally a subjective one, with personal opinion being frequently expressed (various examples can be found in the last three paragraphs). Paragraph five could be described as objective, where the writer balances negative and positive views about the shop and its owner.

WRITING IN FOCUS 3

The Dangling Man (Pages 74–76)

*What do you notice about the **structure** of the first three sentences? How effective is it as the opening of a review of a mountaineering book?*

> The first sentence is repeated with a new piece added on each time. (This is known as 'incremental repetition'.) As the sentences get longer each time, this gives the effect of progression, or even climbing, which is suitable for a book on mountaineering.

*The word 'schadenfreude' means enjoying someone else's misfortune. How might the **context** have told you this?*

> The word 'thrill' suggests enjoyment. What gives him this feeling is that while he is safe, 'lying down', he is reading of the risks of mountaineers who are in an 'alarming' position, and 'in imminent danger of falling . . . to certain death'.

*Can you show how the first sentence in this paragraph acts as a **link**?*

> The phrase 'from this almost subterranean perspective' refers to his reading mountaineering books while lying down. The rest of the sentence introduces one particular book, *Touching the Void*, by Joe Simpson, which he goes on to discuss.

*In paragraph 3, the reviewer compares this book with an earlier one by the same author. He combines a slightly **tongue-in-cheek** tone with a more **serious** one in which he expresses genuine admiration. Can you pick out a phrase which is an example of each? (Make clear which is which.)*

> Tongue-in-cheek expressions: a particularly nasty little 6,000 metre peak; following the ascent . . . came the descent; somewhat swifter than planned.

> Serious expressions: a minor classic; tautly described and dangerous in the extreme; heroically belayed him down.

*Comment on the **metaphor** in the last two sentences of this paragraph. Why is it particularly suitable to use for a book on this topic?*

> He compares the suspense in the two books to a tense or slack rope. The first book he found very tense as a taut and frozen rope would be; the second book does not maintain the suspense well which he compares to the 'slack feel' of a rope which is not being stretched. The metaphor is clear and easy to understand, and it is appropriate because ropes are an essential part of mountaineering equipment.

In what way do you think lack of imagination might contribute to an impression of courage?

What might appear to be bravery might be merely a failure to imagine and anticipate sensibly the real risks of the project.

Can you write down in your own words the aspect of mountaineering that the author says has 'such a compelling hold' on our imaginations? Do you agree with him?

We are amazed at the fact that mountaineers are consciously willing to risk their lives for the love of their sport. Most readers would agree with the author, since they would not share this willingness to take immense risks.

*What is the **tone** of the first sentence of this paragraph?*

Ironic / mocking / facetious / sarcastic, etc.

Can you explain the author's contrasting thoughts towards the risks Simpson takes which he personifies as 'the little angel on my right shoulder' and 'the little devil on my left'?

The 'good' and responsible side of his personality was glad when Simpson gave up on something that might have led him into life-threatening danger. However, his 'bad' or irresponsible side was disappointed, as he was cheated of the excitement of reading about the dangers.

*Comment on the **choice of words** used in Simpson's title,* Storms of Silence.

It is an example of oxymoron, as the ideas in 'storms' and 'silence' appear to contradict each other. The contrast conveys both the wildness and the isolation of the mountains. Simpson also uses alliteration. The 's' sound might be appropriate for either quietness or the sound of the wind for 'storms'.

Why does the reviewer object to Simpson choosing the phrase Storms of Silence *as the title for his book?*

The silence of the great mountains is part of their awe-inspiring appeal. However, the reviewer feels Simpson does not appreciate this since he listens to music on his Walkman as he climbs. The reviewer could have accepted suitably dignified, classical music, but he is disappointed to learn that Simpson prefers loud pop music which would destroy the atmosphere, and certainly makes the book title inappropriate.

Can you identify at least two purposes the writer had in writing this review? Give evidence for these. Rank them in order of importance, giving your reasons.

1. Discussing the book critically / giving information on the book / comparing this book with a previous one by the same author.

    He passes judgement on the book in the last three paragraphs: 'slack feel'; 'lack of imagination'; 'bound to disappoint'. These phrases are examples of his criticism which is mainly negative. In the last two paragraphs he explains what happens in the book: 'Simpson gave up on peak after peak', etc. He begins by describing the earlier book's merits and then compares it with the new one in paragraph four. The reviewer believes the earlier one was better because in it 'Simpson confined himself to the technicalities.'

2. Writing a humorous / entertaining article.
    He uses many witty language techniques like the incremental repetition in paragraph one or the rope metaphor in paragraph four. He uses irony throughout with humorous effect: 'What he's really good at . . . is falling off them.'

    * Rank order is a matter of personal opinion: either choice is valid and acceptable if adequately supported.

    Possible responses: The aspect of entertainment is more important because the author is as much concerned with himself as with the book: he amuses us at some length with his personal views on reading about risk-takers.

    Or: The review aspect is more important as the author does seriously assess the book's merits, albeit in a humorous way. The reader can find guidance about whether or not the book is worth reading.

The writer has used a very personal and humorous style for his review, rather than a straighter, more serious one. Consider why a more serious approach might be preferred by some readers. Which style would appeal to you more, and why?

A more serious approach might be preferred by mountaineers or enthusiasts of the genre who could be irritated by the self-conscious language devices and also the facetious tone with which Will Self describes serious and life-threatening experiences. Instead of the highly personal introduction, they might prefer more hard facts about the content. To some extent mountaineering itself is mocked.

WRITING IN FOCUS 4

Idol Thoughts (Pages 77–79)

*Do you know the **literal** meaning of the word reincarnated? Use a dictionary to find it if necessary. In what way can Marilyn Monroe be said to have been 'reincarnated' after her death?*

Literally, it means reborn, or brought back to life.

Because her image is everywhere on posters, magazine covers, etc., as if she were alive.

What two aspects of Monroe's character does this quotation illustrate?

The 'dumb blonde' and the comedienne.

*How does the **context** help you explain the word 'epitomised'?*

'Epitomised' means summed up. The word 'typical' shows it was a very apt quotation. The fact that the remark is so stupid, but endearing and funny sums up the characteristics of the 'dumb blonde'.

The 'American Dream' is the belief that in the United States, anyone can become rich and successful, no matter who they are or where they come from. Was Marilyn Monroe living proof of this?

She was a good example as she became one of the top film stars of her day, with all the money and fame that goes with this, but her origins were very humble.

In the last sentence of this paragraph Marilyn Monroe is referred to as a 'goddess'. Can you find two words in the first paragraph which also show her being regarded in this way? Can you explain your choice?

'cult' (line 1): a cult involves worship.

'mythic' (line 2): many myths are stories of supernatural characters like gods and goddesses.

're-incarnated' (line 2) suggests the magic or supernatural power associated with a goddess.

Using a dictionary if necessary, explain the phrase 'iconic status'.

The condition of being regarded as an object of worship

*Constance Collier uses a 'humming-bird' **image** to describe the actress. What special qualities of Marilyn do you think this captures?*

Her beauty / fragility / rarity.

*Show how the first sentence in this paragraph has a **linking** function.*

The word 'mystique' refers back to the mysterious aura of Monroe discussed earlier and suggested by the religious references and the humming-bird image; 'vulnerability' or the fact that she was easily harmed is the idea which is explored in the discussion that follows of her troubled background.

In your own words, explain why the author believes Monroe appeals particularly to 'mixed-up adolescents.'

She appeals because she also seemed to have parents who let her down, something many adolescents feel. She was known to be lonely, another common factor. However, her stardom also appeals to young people, many of whom fantasise about having glamorous lives in the future.

How, according to the author, has Monroe's early death contributed to her continuing popularity?

It creates a legend, like that of James Dean, of Marilyn being too good to live. It is intriguing since we don't know how her life might have turned out.

What do you understand by 'teenage angst'? Use a dictionary if necessary.

Anxiety about the human condition, which is particularly strong in young people.

In this paragraph the author makes a comparison with the Queen. What is gained by it, do you think?

The contrast is very striking as Marilyn is still in our minds a beautiful blonde while the Queen is a plain, elderly woman. Since both are the same age, this shows how Marilyn has been suspended in time, and immortalised. Since the Queen's image is also very well known, the contrast is easy to appreciate.

How effective do you find the imagery in this paragraph?

'Caught in aspic' is a food image, and suggests something delicious preserved. This captures both her lasting quality and her attractiveness. The simile 'like a beautiful butterfly in a glass case' is even more striking. A butterfly pinned in a case is dead but retains its fragile beauty. There is also possibly a connotation of pain. 'Frozen' also suggests the idea of suspended animation as Marilyn's image transcends her death.

*In your own words, give **two** pieces of evidence which show women admired Monroe as well as men. Explain the reasons for this.*

1. She appeals to feminists as she was badly treated by men, and wanted to be treated seriously.
2. Many women have imitated her looks, which shows how much they admire her style.
3. Other film-stars, including some of her contemporaries and more recent ones like Madonna, have become successful through imitating her.

Which piece of evidence mentioned in the article do you feel provides the most convincing proof of Monroe's continuing appeal? Explain why.

Any reasonable answer, which might include the reference to the vast amounts of 'Marilyn' merchandise still being sold, the number of stars who continue to ape her style.

The author uses a pun in the title of this article. Can you explain the two meanings? How appropriate do you find the pun?

Idol as it is spelt means an icon, which Marilyn was, so the title may mean thoughts about such a person. The pun is on 'idle': idle thoughts are reflections of a random or casual kind, which describes the tone and style of this piece of reflective writing. The two meanings are therefore appropriate and the pun is thus apt and witty.

PART 3 — INTERPRETATION PRACTICE

INTERPRETATION PRACTICE (1)

The Status of Women (Pages 81–86)

Passage One

(a) *'Bolt-on accessory'; 'ghettoise.' What idea is common to both of these images? Comment in detail on the effectiveness of one of them.*

Both convey the idea of an added-on extra, something being separate from the mainstream.
(1 mark)

Detailed comment on one of these images for two marks — e.g., a ghetto is a place where an unwelcome section of the population is forced to live away from the majority. This implies that by devoting separate chapters to women in their books the historians are in effect relegating women to a 'ghetto' in history.

Total for question: 3 marks

(b) *By referring to the author's word choice, comment on the contrast in style and tone between paragraphs four and five.*

Paragraph 4: formal / serious / factual / discursive / analytical tone.   (1 mark)
Reference to expressions such as 'strictly delineated', 'spheres of activity', etc.   (1 mark)
Paragraph 5: informal / colloquial / conversational tone.   (1 mark)
Reference to 'sorry, lassies', 'the rest of you', parenthesis of 'we've got a nice graph on that one', etc.   (1 mark)

Total for question: 4 marks

(c) *Comment on the tone of 'Sorry lassies, say the historians, but you've got to face facts'.*

Humorous / flippant / mock-apologetic.   (1 mark)
Reference to 'lassies' (i.e., young girls) as patronising, etc.   (1 mark)

Total for question: 2 marks

(d) *Explain how the sentence 'This is just not the full picture' provides a linking function in the argument.*

'This' points back to the view of women's role outlined in the previous paragraph, (1 mark) while the rest of the sentence implies that the following paragraph will seek to give 'the full picture'.   (1 mark)

Total for question: 2 marks

(e) *Comment on the sentence structure of lines 29–35.*

Both sentences follow a similar pattern: both are in question form; both begin with 'what about' followed by the name of an individual woman and details of her courageous acts.

Total for question: 2 marks

(f) *Explain how the examples of Anne Leith and Anne McKay contribute to the author's argument.*

Both show that not all women were at home 'stirring the porridge' by giving examples of how some played a role in military and social affairs.

Total for question: 2 marks

(g) (i) *What does the author believe that historians should aim to do?*

Paraphrase of 'strive to see the whole picture from as many points of view as possible'.

(1 mark)

(ii) *What two factors might hold the historians back in achieving this aim?*

Paraphrase of 'his or her prejudices, such as 'preconceived opinions, not based on an examination of the facts';
(1 mark)
and 'cultural conditioning', such as 'judging past events according to the standards / points of view of his / her own times'.
(1 mark)

Total for question: 3 marks

Passage Two

(h) *Explain the use of two features of the punctuation in the opening sentence.*

Use of a dash to introduce an elaboration of the previous statement.   (1 mark)
Use of a colon to introduce a list.   (1 mark)

Total for question: 2 marks

(i) (i) *What is the single main contrast suggested between the various locations listed in lines 6–7?*

Contrast between simpler ways of life (fields / village markets / the home) and more complex, sophisticated urban / industrial life (factories / supermarkets / board rooms). Answers would need to give both sides of the contrast.

(ii)   *How does the sentence structure reinforce this contrast?*

Grouping the locations in pairs (1 mark) emphasises how these locations are opposites.   (1 mark)

Total for question: 4 marks

(j)   *Look again at the sentence in lines 22–25 ('At this very moment . . . running countries').*
       Comment on the order in which the various examples are arranged.

Build up to climax.   (1 mark)
Begins with the basic biological and domestic roles performed by women and ends with the high profile, public ones.   (1 mark)

Total for question: 2 marks

(k)   *Look at lines 26–31. In your own words, summarise the problems faced by women in some parts of the world.*

      6 x ½ mark for the following points:
            — dying from illnesses which could have been cured;
            — having to watch their children starve;
            — not being given an education;
            — having to turn to prostitution;
            — being unable to borrow money;
            — being denied the right to vote.

Some slight attempt to use own words would be expected.

Total for question: 3 marks

(l)   *Give an example of how the speech argues that an improvement in the status of women would benefit the rest of society.*

Lines 17–19 and 38–39 provide suitable examples.

Total for question: 2 marks

(m)   *In your own words, explain three ways in which families rely on women (lines 37–40).*

Paraphrase of 'emotional support and care' (½ mark),'labour in the home' (½ mark) and extra income (½ mark) needed to raise healthy children and care for other relatives (½ mark).

Total for question: 2 marks

Questions on both passages

(n) *What similarities do you notice between the role of women in history, considered in passage one, and the status of women as outlined in passage two?*

Any valid points, such as: both writers argue, in different ways, that women's full potential in society has not been fully realised; both writers concentrate on the role of ordinary women rather than the 'great and powerful', etc.

Total for question: 3 marks

(o) *Examine the various methods used by each writer to persuade the reader. Which do you consider more successful? Why?*

Answers should focus on technique here, and comments should be backed up with quotations.

Persuasive techniques in passage one include rhetorical questions, use of individual case histories to prove general points, parenthesis, humorous tone, etc.

Passage two uses repetition of sentence structure (e.g., paragraph three), listing effects building up to a climax, personal pronoun ('we') to appeal to and involve reader, etc.

Total for question: 4 marks

INTERPRETATION PRACTICE (2)

Novels (Pages 87–90)

Passage One

(a) In the first paragraph (lines 1–6), what two things about reading does the author see as amazing?

The reader can immediately obtain information from the arrangement of printed letters on the page.   (1 mark)

It is not necessary to read the words aloud; the eye can assimilate the information.
                                                                                                        (1 mark)

Total for question: 2 marks

(b) In paragraph 2 (lines 7–14), what does the author see as the main advantage of print in book form?

Its convenience (1 mark). The information is contained in a compact form (½ mark) which can be carried around (½ mark).

Total for question: 2 marks

(c) Look at paragraphs 2, (lines 7–14), and 6 (lines 34–43). Explain in your own words the difference between 'good' and 'bad' books, according to the author.

'Good' books are harder to read. They are serious literature, such as the novels of Sir Walter Scott, whose prose style seems heavy going to many modern readers.   (2 marks)
'Bad' books are easier to read. They are enjoyable and do not tax the intellect.   (2 marks)

Total for question: 4 marks

(d) Look at paragraph 3 (lines 15–21). Choose either the first or second of the author's father's 'three tips'. Briefly state it in your own words, then give reasons why you do or do not think it good advice.

Do not try to read more than two books at one time.   (1 mark)

Two marks for a reasonable explanation either for or against the advice: e.g., this is *good* advice as it would not be possible to sustain interest in more than two books; one would tend to forget and lose interest since there would be gaps while the books remained unread; it would spoil one's enjoyment of a book if one could not find out what happened at once. Alternatively, it could reasonably be seen as *bad* advice: e.g., one might be in a mood for a different type of book at different points in the day; some avid readers might be able to cope with more than two at a time.   (2 marks)

OR

If you get as far as page 36 it is worth finishing a book. (1 mark)

Two marks for any reasonable explanation either way: e.g., good advice, as if you have invested so much time it would be a waste not to give the book a chance; bad advice in that a book might begin promisingly but turn out to be very dull and would thus be a waste of time. (2 marks)

Total for question: 3 marks.

(e) *Show how the opening sentence of paragraph 4, 'This last injunction . . . outrageous', acts as a link.*

The expression 'this last injunction' refers to the final piece of advice, namely to make marginal notes. (1 mark)

The words 'will seem to many people outrageous' leads on to a discussion of whether it is shocking to write on a book. (1 mark)

Total for question: 2 marks

(f) *Look at paragraph 4 (lines 22–27). In your own words, explain how the author justifies his habit of making notes in books.*

In later years he can reread his own comments and recall his enjoyment of various aspects of the book. (2 marks)

Others may read his comments and enjoy being directed to, e.g., a funny story or a good quotation. (2 marks)

Total for question: 4 marks

(g) *'A book should never be defaced by the reader's stupid comments.' (lines 22–23). Describe the author's tone here, explaining your answer.*

The author's tone is ironic / sarcastic / tongue-in-cheek / mocking. (1 mark)

The italics stress the misplaced outrage of those who disagree with writing on books. It is a kind of parody. (1 mark)

Total for question: 2 marks

(h) *What clue does the author give in paragraph 5 (lines 28–33) which explains his love of reading?*

Any two of the following.

The author describes the feeling of looking forward to going early to bed in order to continue with an enjoyable book. (1 mark)

He treats the characters as if they were real people, and wishes to 'meet' them again. (1 mark)

He feels he knows the characters in the books better than real people. (1 mark)

Total for question: 2 marks

(i) *Explain the tone of the words 'spooky' and 'soapy' (line 42) to describe music on taped books. What is revealed of the author's attitude to such background music?*

The words are colloquial which creates a contemptuous, disparaging tone.   (1 mark)

The author dislikes it, finding it clichéd and predictable.   (1 mark)

Total for question: 2 marks

(j) *What is the effect of the final short sentence in the last paragraph?*

Any reasonably developed comment for two marks, e.g., it has a humorous impact, its simplicity contrasts with the pretentious comment of the woman about reading *Anna Karenina* in Russian.   (2 marks)

Total for question: 2 marks

Passage Two

(k) *Jane Austen shows an awareness of Nigel Nicolson's distinction between 'good books' and 'bad books'. Give an example of each from Passage 2, making clear which is which.*

'Good', i.e., difficult or tedious books would include *The History of England*; an anthology including the poetry of Milton, Pope and Prior and selections from *The Spectator* and Sterne.   (1 mark)

'Bad', i.e., entertaining books, would include novels such as *Cecilia, Camilla* or *Belinda*.   (1 mark)

Total for question: 2 marks

(l) *Comment on the language technique used, and its effect, in the phrase 'the nine-hundredth abridger of* The History of England' .

Hyperbole (exaggeration).   (1 mark)

Effect is ironic / humorous.   (1 mark)

Total for question: 2 marks

(m) (i) *Explain the author's tone in the expression 'performances which have only genius, wit, and taste to recommend them' (lines 9–10).*

Irony.   (1 mark)

Total for question: 1 mark

(ii) *Give another example of this tone from the passage.*

It is only *Cecilia*, etc. / only some work in which the greatest powers of the mind are displayed.   (1 mark)

Total for question: 1 mark

(n) *In the last paragraph (lines 16–22), the author presents five features of great novels. List these in your own words.*

A display of great intellect;
accurate character analysis;
a great variety of characters;
bright, entertaining and humorous writing;
good style.

(1 mark for each point made without using the original wording of the passage)

Total for question: 5 marks

Questions on Both Passages

(p) *Using quotation to support your answer, compare and contrast the style of the two passages. You should consider the author's purpose, sentence structure, word choice and tone. (Remember to include similarities as well as differences.)*

Purpose: Passage one is reflective: 'When you come to think of it'; personal: 'I can rediscover . . .'. Passage two is persuasive / argumentative: it is pressing the point that novels and novelists deserve respect: 'work . . . in which the greatest powers of the mind are displayed'. It is slightly personal, as the author uses 'our' showing she is a novelist herself, but she doesn't confide in the reader to the extent the first writer does.

Sentence structure: Passage one is fairly colloquial, with many short sentences, abbreviations, 'didn't'; and exclamations: 'What a convenient thing a book is!' There are some longer, more complex sentences. It ends in a short sentence which produces an anticlimax: 'I didn't'. Passage two has much longer, more complex sentences; it is written more formally, but it also includes a section of direct speech: 'Oh! It is only a novel', by way of illustration. It also includes the informal 'Now' which introduces a final exclamation which produces a climax.

Word choice: Passage one uses modern and fairly colloquial language: 'kids'; the informal 'you'; 'on the go'. Passage two uses more formal, literary vocabulary: 'eulogised'; 'affected indifference'. It also has some archaic usages: 'It is really very well for a novel'.

Tone: Passage one is light-hearted and chatty: 'what do I care?' It is almost gossipy: 'there was a terrible woman'. It is humorous: 'big slabs of prose'. Passage two is more ironic: 'It is only a novel . . .' It also shows humour, with an ironic, gently mocking, note: 'had the same young lady been engaged . . . how proudly would she have produced the book.'

Four clear points of contrast or comparison, supported by quotation, should be made from at least two of these areas.

Total for question: 4 marks

Total for Paper: 40 marks

INTERPRETATION PRACTICE (3)

Grandmothers (Pages 91–95)

Passage One

(a) *Animal images are frequently used to describe the 'grannies' in paragraphs 1, 2 and 3. Pick out two examples, each from a different paragraph. Explain what impression each of the images conveys to you, making clear whether you find them pleasant or unpleasant.*

One mark for each of two correctly identified images (each to be from a different paragraph); one mark for a reasonable comment on each.

'like mice in the walls' (para. 1): pleasant, as mice are small and fragile; / unpleasant, as mice are vermin and many people hate them.
'a tiny white shrew' (para. 2): pleasant, as it suggests something small, fair and delicate; / unpleasant, as shrews are associated with meanness, nagging, etc.
'frugal as a sparrow' (para. 3): pleasant, as a sparrow is an attractive, perky, self-sufficient little bird; / unpleasant, since it suggests something common and plain.
'simple . . . as a grub' (para. 3): unpleasant, as it suggests a maggot, rather inhuman and disgusting in form.

Total for question: 4 marks

(b) *Explain how the first sentence of paragraph 3 (lines 15–16) forms a link between paragraphs 2 and 3.*

The phrase 'small indulgences' refers back to the pleasures in life which kept Granny Wallon happy, such as her wines. (1 mark)

'Had none of them' introduces the description of Granny Trill's more spartan life style. (1 mark)

Total for question: 2 marks

(c) *Comment on the structure of the sentence, 'She was continually . . . fungoid dust' (lines 30–32). Say what effect you think the author was trying to achieve.*

The author uses a large number of verbs ending in 'ing'. This list emphasises the complicated ritual involved in taking the snuff. (1 mark)

It is a long sentence, leading up to the phrase 'an explosion of fungoid dust' which creates a slightly humorous climax to the procedure. (1 mark)

Total for question: 2 marks

(d) Look at paragraph 6 (lines 33–37). 'The snuff-box repelled . . . witchery'.
Explain how the choice of vocabulary and imagery accurately convey the boys' feelings of both repulsion and excitement.

Repulsion: 'reeking' implies a disgusting smell; / 'of the underworld', 'dust of decay', 'powdered flesh', 'crushed old bones', 'rubbish of graves' (one example required) are all associated with death / 'rust-scrapings' implies something decaying. (Any two quotes + comments for two marks.)

Excitement: 'this fearful spice', 'sharp and stinging', 'animating the air', 'tingling fumes' all suggest something stimulating; / 'secret breath of witchery' suggests excitement (but might also be justified under 'repulsion') (Any two quotes + comments for 2 marks.)

Total for question: 4 marks

(e) How does the sentence in brackets in the last paragraph (lines 43–44) affect your response to the passage as a whole, and its view of 'grannies'?

There are many possible answers which should be judged on merit. E.g., it reminds us that this was a child's view. It may seem over imaginative and whimsical but this is typical of a child's thinking. It may make us realise this is an antiquated picture, not applicable to today. It may create a tone of nostalgia.

Total for question: 2 marks

Passage Two

(f) (i) 'granny-battering' (line 1). From where do you think the author has derived this word?

It is formed by analogy with 'wife-battering' or 'baby-battering'.   (1 mark)

(ii) What effect do you think this expression has on the reader?

It is humorous as it sounds unlikely, but at the same time informative as we readily understand the more common terms.   (2 marks)

Total for question: 3 marks

(g) Comment on the sentence structure of the last sentence of paragraph 1 (lines 6–9): "But what is much more common . . . years". Explain how the structure chosen is appropriate to the ideas.

It is a very long, loosely structured sentence, ending with a series of adverbial phrases.
          (1 mark)

The structure is appropriate as it emphasises the long, dreary task of caring for an elderly person for years without any respite.   (1 mark)

Total for question: 2 marks

(h) *Look at the opening sentence of paragraph 2: 'If it is your own old Mum . . . children.' There is a contrast in style between the phrases 'your own old Mum' and 'with impunity'. Explain the contrast, and say what effect the author achieves by using the two styles throughout the passage.*

'your own old Mum' is colloquial.   (1 mark)
'with impunity' is formal.   (1 mark)
The colloquialisms give the writing an ironic humour and make it very accessible, while the formal expressions remind us of the seriousness of the issue.   (1 mark)

Total for question: 3 marks

(i) *In paragraph 2 (lines 10–17), caring for the elderly is seen as less stressful for professional carers than for relatives. What reasons are suggested for this?*

A professional carer does it for a fixed amount of time whereas the family member has a never-ending task;   (1 mark)
a professional carer does not have to accept abuse whereas a family member may have to;   (1 mark)
a professional leaves the problem person behind at the end of the shift and returns to his or her normal life which the family member cannot do;   (1 mark)
the professional is not emotionally involved and thus is not subject to feelings of guilt or liable to emotional blackmail as the family member may be.   (1 mark)
(Any three of these reasons.)

Total for question: 3 marks

(j) *Look at paragraph 3 (lines 18–23). Explain the difference in the perceived roles of men and women in caring for the elderly.*

Men assume it is not their job. It is assumed that women will be willing to do this work 'for free'. Men see this as quite reasonable ('nodded approvingly'). (2 marks for reasonably developed answer.)

Total for question: 2 marks

(k) *Sum up in your own words, in formal continuous prose, the main features of the author's scheme for providing care for the elderly.*

It would be a voluntary scheme; / it could be made a condition for receiving 5–10 years of the old-age pension; / it would be part-time only; / it would be done in good conditions; / service would only be done in addition to the help of professional carers. (Any 4 points clearly made.)

Total for question: 4 marks

Questions on Both Passages

(l)   The passages offer two different attitudes towards the elderly. Referring to the word choice of both passages, sum up the two attitudes, and say which is closer to your own view, giving brief reasons.

Passage one: writer's attitude is generally positive. The grannies are respectfully called 'old ladies'. Granny Wallon's skills in raising many children and making 'excellent' wines are admired. Granny Trill's snuff-box is seen as quite exciting, with its 'tingling fumes'. There is regret in the comment that grannies like this are not seen today. He says they 'enthralled' him which suggests he is fascinated. His whimsical idea of the parade of grandmas is affectionate and admiring as he prefers them to the guardsmen. There are just a few signs of disgust in the comparison of Granny Trill to a 'grub', the description of her toothless gums, and the repulsive images connected with her snuff. The fact they were the 'images of witches' could also be seen as negative.

Passage two: writer's attitude is totally negative. The elderly are seen as a burden on their families who may even be driven to violence. The old are seen as 'demanding' and 'cantankerous' and imposing an often intolerable strain on their families who are 'driven to the end of their tether'. Old women are seen to 'bully' their daughters, and they are accused of 'emotional blackmail'. The second writer sums up caring for the elderly in strongly emotive language as 'a nightmare of never-ending obligation'. This makes it sound totally joyless.

For each passage at least three of the above quotations and pertinent comments should be given.   (3 marks)
A personal response, reasonably developed, should present candidate's own experience.
                                                                                          (1 mark)

Total for question: 4 marks

(m) Referring closely to the text of both passages, sum up what you see as the problems that might arise when caring for the elderly within the family.

Passage one: Elderly people may have revolting habits like Granny Trill's of 'sliding her folded gums together' and taking snuff, a 'reeking' substance. This would be disgusting to the other family members. An old person losing track of time, like Granny Trill, with her eccentric system of getting up at four in the morning and going to bed again at five in the afternoon, would not fit in with the usual working hours of a family. (Two clearly made points, supported by precise evidence for 2 marks.)

Passage two: Old people may be demanding and bad-tempered; 'cantankerous'. They may treat the family carer badly and there is little such a relative can do: 'can be beastly to you with impunity'; 'bully'. They may create a strain through arousing guilt feelings by using emotional blackmail. Very often men do not feel they are involved and so the burden of caring may fall on a daughter alone. (Two clearly made points, supported by precise evidence for 2 marks.)

Total for question: 4 marks

Total for paper: 40 marks

INTERPRETATION PRACTICE (4)

America and the Americans (Pages 96–100)

Marking Scheme

Passage One

(a) *What does the author state the main purpose of the passage to be?*

Purpose is to define the characteristics which are more common among the American people compared with others.   (1 mark)

Half a mark if the word 'qualities' was taken to mean 'good points' rather than aspects, characteristics, etc.

'to show what Americans are like' would be too vague — 0.

Total for question: 1 mark

(b) *Basing your answer on lines 7 and 8, explain the author's reasons for mentioning the fact that 'the ordinary dwelling is called not a house but a home'.*

'Home' suggests not merely the building but the closeness of the family which lives there.
                                                                                                (1 mark)
This in turn shows the importance of the family as the basis on which society is founded.
                                                                                                (1 mark)

Total for question: 2 marks

(c) *What is meant by a 'nomad race' (line 9)? Explain how the context of the phrase helps you to arrive at the meaning.*

Definition of a 'nomad race' — moving from place to place, no settled base.   (1 mark)
Context: quotation / reference to lines 9–10 ('It is true that they are very ready to shift their camp').   (1 mark)
Reference plus some attempt to pick up connotations of individual words like 'shift' or 'camp' would gain a further mark.

Total for question: 3 marks

(d) *Look at lines 16–19. Explain ONE of the effects the love of 'domesticity' had on American literature.*

Most pupils would probably choose line 17 ('a sentimentality which makes a too crude frontal attack on the emotions') rather than the second half of the sentence in lines 18–19 ('produced as a reaction a not less sentimental toughness').

The first part could be paraphrased as an approach which appeals to the reader's feelings by giving a simplified, romantic view of family life which emphasises only the happy side. (Two marks for a good paraphrase; 1 mark for a poorer attempt, or one which relies too heavily on words from the passage).

Total for question: 2 marks

(e) (i) *Explain the distinction between 'duty' and 'instinct' (line 26).*

Duty: what one is required to do. There is no choice in the matter.   (1 mark)
Instinct: a natural desire to do something — no need to be told to do it.   (1 mark)

(ii) *Which of the examples given makes this distinction particularly clear?*

Example from line 27 of the squatter helping the stranger is appropriate as the phrase 'would never dream he is doing anything unusual' clearly shows the 'instinctive' nature of the act.   (2 marks)

Total for question: 4 marks

(f) *'No doubt this friendliness, since it is an established custom, has its false side' (line 33). Explain how this sentence provides a linking function in the development of the argument of the passage.*

'This friendliness' points back to the topic of the previous paragraph,   (1 mark)

while 'has its false side' introduces the opposite argument of which examples are given in the paragraph which follows.   (1 mark)

Total for question: 2 marks

(g) *What evidence is there in the last paragraph for the author's belief that the Americans are 'fundamentally modest'?*

Americans take note of criticism (½ mark) whereas the vain do not care for other people's views.   (½ mark)

They have the ability to laugh at themselves (½ mark) which those who are not modest cannot do.   (½ mark)

They can accurately pinpoint their own weaknesses and make fun of them (1 mark): paraphrase of 'shrewdest and most ribald critics'.

Total for question: 3 marks

(h) *The author tends to explain his view of contemporary Americans in terms of their ancestors. Using your own words, illustrate this comment by reference to one example from the extract.*

1 mark for suitable example; 1 mark for brief reference to similar characteristics being seen in contemporary Americans or 2 marks for further comment which explains the connection between ancestors and present-day Americans more fully.

Suitable evidence is contained in lines 9–16 and 21–28.

Total for question: 3 marks

Passage Two

(i)   *Comment on the effectiveness of the metaphor 'the mask has dropped from the face' (lines 17–18) and show how this relates to the ideas contained in the second paragraph.*

The metaphor relates to these ideas as it emphasises the difference between outward appearance and reality.   (1 mark)

It is effective because it suggests that the truth has been hidden from people (1 mark), illustrated by examples such as the 'defiant assertions of new buildings' concealing economic instability, or apparently healthy joggers in reality being frightened of violent attacks (1 mark).

Total for question: 3 marks

(j)   (i)   *Explain in your own words what it was that immigrants to America shared in the first period of mass migration.*

Paraphrase of 'aspirations of struggle and self-improvement' — i.e., the desire (1 mark) to work hard to gain a better quality of life (1 mark).

(ii)   *Explain the change which the writer claims has occurred amongst present-day immigrants.*

See line 28: change from bringing their skills to bringing their guile — i.e., instead of offering abilities which contribute to society (1 mark), they adopt a crafty, deceitful approach.   (1 mark)

(iii)   *Quote an expression which reveals the writer's attitude to these more recent immigrants.*

'in the worst sense' or 'as if to recall a better-motivated American'.   (1 mark)

Total for question: 5 marks

(k)   *Explain why Ellis Island would be effective as 'a symbol to uplift New York.'*

Reference to significance of the island in the past.   (1 mark)

This would remind present-day Americans of the determination and sense of purpose that their ancestors had and may therefore inspire them to follow their example.   (1 mark)

Total for question: 2 marks

(l) *Comment on either the structure or imagery of the final sentence and discuss its effectiveness as an ending.*

   Structure: incomplete sentence — emphasises writer's cynicism, creates tension, or similar comment.

   Imagery: 'Big Apple' image used to convey the notion of corruption from within.

   Effectiveness as an ending: sums up writer's view that so much of New York's prosperity and confidence is superficial, concealing the corruption and fear which lies beneath the surface.

   Either 1 mark for structure / imagery and 2 for effectiveness, or vice versa.

   Total for question: 3 marks

Questions on Both Passages

(m) *Note that the question asked about how the writers* present the subject, *suggesting that their* attitude *should be considered. The best answers will therefore not simply list similarities / differences between the passages but will comment on the authors' approach.*

   E.g., *John Buchan* (passage one) takes a general overview of American society; his approach tends to be sympathetic and positive; he stresses the strengths of the American character.

   John Cunningham (passage two) gives a more specific view of present-day New York life; his approach tends to be negative and even cynical; he emphasises fear, insecurity, etc.

   Note the requirement that candidates should use quotations to illustrate their comments

   Total for question: 4 marks

(n) Candidates may, of course, favour either passage one or passage two, but must make reference to *both*, drawing parallels / contrasts to show why they are convinced by one rather than the other. Again, close reference / quotation is required.

   Total for question: 3 marks

   Total for paper: 40 marks

APPENDIX: GRAMMAR AND SYNTAX

Sentences, Clauses and Phrases. (Page 103)

Subject	Verb	Direct Object	Indirect Object	Adverbial Phrase
I	told	a story	the children	
The light	shone			into the room
The aircraft	crashed			just after take-off
She	found	the missing money		in the tea-caddy

WORD ORDER: *Inversion* (Page 104)

Consider what effect is obtained in the following examples of inversion. (The conventional word order is given first for purposes of comparison.) Remember there will only be a slight difference, perhaps of tone or emphasis.

1. (a) His fist smacked down onto the table.
    (b) Down smacked his fist onto the table.

    In example *(b)*, placing the stressed word 'down' at the beginning of the sentence has the effect of onomatopoeia because of the 'd' sound. It imitates the thud of the fist on the wood. In the normal word order, a less heavily stressed, softer sounding word, 'his', begins the sentence which would not have this effect.

2. (a) The car door opened and the Queen stepped out.
    (b) The car door opened and out stepped the Queen.

    Keeping the subject till last in the second clause of the sentence creates a climax. The reader is kept waiting to find out who stepped out and is surprised. In the normal word order this suspense and surprise is lacking.

3. (a) A beautiful princess lived in a dark and gloomy castle in the middle of a dense forest.
    (b) In the middle of a dense forest, in a dark and gloomy castle, lived a beautiful princess.

    Sentence *(b)*, in which the verb and subject are delayed till the end after a number of phrases, is typical of story-telling. The listener is kept in suspense before finding out who lives in the place which is gradually described. Suspense keeps the reader enthralled.

4. (a) I have never done that.
    (b) That, I have never done.

    In example *(b)*, stress is thrown onto the word 'that'. It makes whatever it refers to sound extremely important and serious. When 'that' is placed last, as in *(a)*, it is relatively unstressed. The action itself assumes much less importance.

5. (a) For Henry Jekyll stood there before my eyes, pale and shaken, and half fainting and groping before him with his hands like a man restored from death!
    (b) For there before my eyes — pale and shaken, and half fainting, and groping before him with his hands like a man restored from death — there stood Henry Jekyll!

    Example *(b)* is the original quotation from R.L. Stevenson's *Dr Jekyll and Mr Hyde*. It is similar in structure to example 3 above. By keeping the main verb and subject till the end of the sentence, aided by an effective use of the dash which delays the end of the sentence further, Stevenson creates a most thrilling climax. The identity of the person follows a list of intriguing descriptive phrases which keep the reader guessing who is being described until the dramatic disclosure at the end of the sentence.

GRAMMAR AND SYNTAX

FOR PRACTICE (Page 108)

Comment on the authors' use of sentence structure in the following pieces of writing and consider their purpose in the techniques they have chosen. You could also comment on any other striking features of style such as word choice or imagery.

1. The word 'action' at the end of the first sentence is followed by a series of sentences containing verbs of action, all following the subject 'he'. The progression of energy expressed by the verbs indicates the character's pent-up frustration: 'took', 'tossed', 'pulled', 'flung', etc. The repetition of 'and' also stresses the restlessness and activity.

    The extract also shows a good use of personification in the first sentence. The simile 'crouched . . . like a depressed relation' adds a touch of black humour and shows how the character finds his surroundings dreary and oppressive.

2. The syntax of these lines is not technically correct. The adverbial clause beginning 'when the sun . . .' is followed rather oddly by a verb in the imperative voice: 'Look up'. This produces a strange, disjointed effect, emphasised by the ellipsis at the end of line 3. In the adverbial clause, the poet builds up a series of phrases, repeating the word 'beyond' in a deliberately protracted line, holding back the verb 'departs' till the start of the next line. This has the effect of stressing the suddenness of the departure of the sun after a long twilight and the sudden darkening which accompanies this.

    The use of the word 'things' and the phrase 'between the day and the night' create an ominous sense of mystery.

3. This extract makes clear use of inversion: 'Back we went', 'down we went'. These emphasise the impression of the characters retracing their steps to look for the lost brooch.

    The frequency of the participles, 'searching', 'following', 'refinding', 'pushing', reinforces the sense of urgency in the search.

4. The repeated use of the passive voice: 'was told', 'it was alleged', 'he was said', 'the alarm was raised', are typical of the impersonal, objective tone of legal proceedings.

    It should be noted how this contrasts with the violence of the subject matter: 'threatened . . . with a knife'.

5. This narrative is written in the 'historic present' tense: 'feels'; 'has'. This lends a heightened sense of drama and immediacy to the story. In the second last sentence there is a series of participial phrases (based on the participles 'littering', 'unfolding', 'shaking') which stress the prolonged nature of the search for the money. The final sentence is a short, bald statement. It gives the appearance of an anti-climax, and in a sense it is, but it actually raises the tension as the search has been in vain. The simplicity of the language makes it all the more hard-hitting.

6. The most noticeable feature of this extract is the enormously long sentences. The second one seems interminable, with a long series of rambling phrases beginning with 'from'. One would expect finally a phrase beginning with 'to' to complete the idea of a range of experiences, but this never arrives. The effect is incoherent and formless.

    The word choice is equally opaque. The list of extremes and superlatives —'extraordinary', 'boundless', incredible', 'greatest', 'endless', etc. — becomes tedious and absurd and ultimately fails to have any effect. There are several grandiloquent phrases which actually mean very little: 'authentic cultural matrix', 'refined facets', etc. The use of imagery is also unselective and overdone. The extended image in line 3: 'tesserae of the wonderful mosaic' is actually quite appropriate in describing the beauty spots which comprise the Sorrento coast. It suggests many beautiful pieces making up a wonderful whole, and mosaic is a typically Italian art form. However, the writer gets bogged down in an excess of metaphors which are much less well chosen. Describing the perfume of the flowers as a 'jewel' is not a helpful comparison, nor is 'the disturbing voice of silence'.

    In this piece of writing the writer is striving much too hard for effect, and in being unselective he becomes almost incomprehensible.

NOTES